AROUND SHETLAND

A PICTURE GUIDE

The Shetland Times Ltd.
Lerwick
2011

First published by The Shetland Times Ltd., 2011.

ISBN 978-1-904746-63-8

British Library Cataloguing-in-Publication Data
A catalogue record for this book is available from the British Library.

Front cover: Clickimin Broch, Lerwick © Georges Dif
Back cover: Walls © Georges Dif

Printed and published by
The Shetland Times Ltd.,
Gremista, Lerwick,
Shetland ZE1 0PX, Scotland.

AROUND SHETLAND

Lerwick

1. Tall Ship at the South End
2. Clickimin Broch
3. Small boat harbour
4. The Market Cross
5. The Lodberries
6. Stormy scene at the Lodberries
7. Albert Wharf
8. NorthLink ferry leaving Lerwick.
9. Up-Helly-A'
10. Up-Helly-A'
11. Up-Helly-A' procession
12. Burning galley, Up-Helly-A'

Central Mainland

13. Grunna Water, South Nesting
14. Stormy seas, South Nesting
15. Aurora Borealis, South Nesting
16. Catfirth
17. Sunset, Lunna
18. Scalloway
19. Eastshore, Scalloway
20. Scalloway
21. Trondra
22. Asta Loch and Tingwall valley
23. Tingwall valley
24. Nesbister Böd, Whiteness
25. Weisdale
26. Voe

West Mainland

27. Sandness

28. Walls
29. Reawick
30. Foula from Walls
31. Kirk Holm, Garderhouse
32. Clousta

South Mainland

33. Cunningsburgh
34. Mousa Broch
35. Sandwick
36. Channerwick
37. Mossy Hill
38. St. Ninian's Isle
39. Shetland ponies at Levenwick
40. Crofthouse Museum
41. Seal pup at Fitful
42. Otter and cub at Boddam
43. Sunset at Boddam
44. Freezing fog at Sumburgh
45. Posing seal
46. Puffin at Sumburgh
47. Killer whale of Sumburgh

North Mainland

48. Brae
49. Busta House
50. Dore Holm
51. Eshaness
52. Eshaness
53. Ronas Voe
54. Turls Head, Northmavine
55. Inner Lees, Hamar

56. Uyea Isle
57. Fitful Head from Ronas Hill
58. Hillswick

Isles

59. Inter-island ferry
60. Burrafirth, Unst
61. Burrafirth, Unst
62. Norwick, Unst
63. Hermaness and Muckle Flugga
64. White Wife, Otterswick, Yell
65. Breckon, Yell
66. The Links, Mid Yell
67. Otter, Yell
68. Tresta, Fetlar
69. Urie Ness, Fetlar
70. Papa Stour
71. Bressay Lighthouse
72. Grindiscol, Bressay
73. Noss cliffs
74. Out Skerries
75. Ferry arriving at Symbister, Whalsay
76. Foula
77. Foula cliffs
78. Biggings, Foula
79. The *New Advance* in her berth, Foula
80. Fair Isle
81. North Haven, Fair Isle
82. Sunset, Fair Isle
83. Fair Isle Bird Observatory
84. Shetland ponies

1. Tall ship at the South End, Lerwick.

2. Clickimin Broch is an iron age broch tower which stands next to the Clickimin Loch in Lerwick.

3. The small boat harbour, Lerwick, with the replica longship *Dim Riv* in the foreground. Lerwick Town Hall can be seen dominating the skyline.

4. The Market Cross, Lerwick.

5. The Lodberries at the South End of Commercial Street. Dating back to the 18th century these houses and warehouses were built by Lerwick's merchants.

© *Georges Dif*

6. Stormy scene at the Lodberries, Lerwick.

© Dave Donaldson

7. Albert Wharf, Lerwick, with visiting tall ship and the Bressay ferry *Leirna* at its berth.

© *Georges Dif*

8. NorthLink ferry *Hjaltland* leaving Lerwick. Taken from Bressay.

9. Lerwick Guizer Jarl's Squad with the galley, Up-Helly-A'.

10. Lerwick Guizer Jarl and squad, Up-Helly-A'.

11. Lerwick Up-Helly-A' torchlit procession.

© *Kenneth Shearer*

12. The burning galley, Up-Helly-A', Lerwick.

© *Kenneth Shearer*

13. Grunna Water, South Nesting.

14. Stormy seas at Gletness, South Nesting.

15. Aurora Borealis above Whalsay looking from Eswick in South Nesting.

16. Rainbow over Catfirth.

17. Sunset, Lunna.

18. The fishing port of Scalloway was Shetland's ancient capital.

© *Georges Dr*

19. Eastshore, Scalloway, featuring Scalloway Castle which was built in 1600 by Earl Patrick Stewart.

20. Scalloway.

21. A snowy Trondra.

22. Asta Loch and Tingwall valley.

23. Tingwall valley through to Burra, with Fitful Head in the distance.

24. Nesbister Böd, Whiteness.

© Dave Donaldson

25. Weisdale.

26. Voe.

27. Clumpers, Sandness.

28. Walls.

29. Reawick photographed from Skeld with the Skeld pier and marina in the foreground.

© *Bruce Wilcock*

30. Foula from Littlelure, Walls.

© Dave Donaldson

31. Kirk Holm, between Garderhouse and Reawick.

© *Viviene Harvey*

32. Clousta.

33. Cunningsburgh.

34. Dating from the Iron Age, Mousa Broch stands over 42 feet high and measures 49 feet at the base.

35. Sandwick.

36. Channerwick.

37. Ruins of a crofthouse on Mossy Hill. Fitful Head, Spiggie Loch and Scousburgh Sands (aka Spiggie Beach) in the background. © *Georges Dif*

38. St. Ninian's Isle and tombolo.

9. Shetland pony mare and foal at Levenwick.

© *Rhonas Thomson*

40. The Crofthouse Museum at Voe, Dunrossness, was built in 1870. Today it offers a glimpse into Shetland life during the 19th century.

© Georges D

41. Seal pup at Fitful.

42. Otter and cub at Boddam.

43. Sunrise at Boddam.

44. Freezing fog at Sumburgh.

45. Posing seal.

46. Puffin at Sumburgh.

47. Killer whale off Sumburgh.

48. Brae.

49. Now operating as a hotel, Busta House is steeped in history. The main building was built in 1714 with the earliest parts dating from 1599.

50. Dore Holm.

51. The remote and rugged coastline of Eshaness.

52. Eshaness lighthouse offers an unrivalled view of the dramatic coastal scenery.

© Dave Donaldson

53. Ronas Voe.

54. Turls Head, Northmavine, with The Crook on the left and the Lang Ayre and Stonga Banks on the right.

55. Inner Lees, Hamar.

56. The tidal island of Uyea.

57. Looking towards Fitful Head from Ronas Hill. © *Bruce Wilcock*

58. Hillswick.

59. A network of inter-island ferries make it quick and easy to travel to and from the outlying isles.

© *Georges Dif*

60. Burrafirth, Unst, viewed from above Saxa Vord.

© Georges Dif

51. Burrafirth, Unst.

62. Norwick, Unst.

53. The most northerly point in Britain. Hermaness and Muckle Flugga rock and lighthouse. The moors and cliffs of Hermaness are home to over 100,000 breeding seabirds.

© *Georges Dif*

64. Da White Wife at Otterswick, Yell. She was the figurehead taken from the *Bohus*, a German sailing vessel wrecked in 1924.

© *Alastair Christie-Johnston*

55. Breckon, Yell.

66. The Links, Mid Yell.

57. Otter with lumpfish, Yell.

© Alastair Christie-Johnston

68. Tresta, Fetlar. © *Colin Gran*

59. Urie Ness, Fetlar.

© *Paul Turner*

70. Papa Stour.

71. Bressay Lighthouse built in 1858 by the famous Stevenson family. Today it is automated and used as holiday accommodation. © *Georges Dif*

72. Grindiscol, Bressay.

73. The cliffs of Noss.

74. Out Skerries lies 24 miles north-east of Lerwick. It consists of three main islands – Housay (in the foreground) which is joined to Bruray by a bridge and the uninhabited island of Grunay.

© *Vivienne Harvey*

75. Inter-island ferry *Hendra* arriving at Symbister, Whalsay.

76. Foula is home to the most isolated community in Britain.

© *Georges Dif*

77. Foula cliffs. In days past the people of Foula were reknowned for their skill in scaling the cliff faces.

© *Georges Dif*

78. Biggings, Foula.

79. The *New Advance* in her berth, Foula.

80. Fair Isle lies midway between Orkney and Shetland.

81. Visiting yachts at North Haven, Fair Isle.

© Dave Wheeler

82. Sunset, Fair Isle.

© Dave Wheeler

33. Fair Isle Bird Observatory.

84. Shetland Ponies.